ROBINSON CRUSOE

BY DANIEL DEFOE

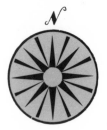

Abridged and adapted by ROBERT LASSON

Illustrated by RON KING

A PACEMAKER CLASSIC

Fearon Publishers, Inc.

Belmont, California

PACEMAKER CLASSICS

Robinson Crusoe
The Moonstone
The Jungle Book
The Last of the Mohicans
Treasure Island
Two Years Before the Mast
20,000 Leagues Under the Sea
Tale of Two Cities

ISBN-0-8224-9225-3

Library of Congress Catalog Card Number: 67-25784

Printed in the United States of America.

Contents

1 I Go to Sea

My name is Robinson Crusoe. I was born in York, England, in 1632. As a boy, I wanted to go to sea. But my father told me that this was not a good way to live. Ships were at sea for many months. Sometimes they were gone for years. Often they were lost and never came home again.

But I didn't care about that. All I wanted was to go to sea. So when I was 19, I ran away from home. I got on a ship going to London. Soon after the ship got under way, a big wind started to blow. The water seemed to go wild. This went on for days. I was very much afraid, and I became very sick. If I ever get on dry land again, I told myself, I'll go straight home. But when I got to London, I did not give it another thought. I signed on a ship and went to sea.

In the next few years, a lot of things happened to me. I was caught by the Turks. But I got away. Then I went to Brazil. I owned a large farm where I grew tobacco. In four years I made a lot of money. But I wanted to go back to

England for a visit. On September 1, 1659, I got on a ship that was to take me back. It was eight years from the day I had run away from home.

The ship was a big one. There were 14 men on it. At first the sun was out. It was very hot. Then, after two weeks, a great storm began. It lasted for 12 days. No one on the ship thought that we would come out alive. The captain did not know what to do. Great waves washed up over the decks. We thought they would break the ship to pieces.

One morning a sailor cried out "Land!" It was an island. The captain headed for the island. But the ship could not make it. We all got into a small boat. We tried to row our way to shore. Then a high wave came and rolled the boat over. I swam toward the shore as well as I could in the high waves. The water washed me on the shore. I was very tired. I climbed over the rocks and sat on the grass. The ship was still being hit by the waves. I looked for other men from the small boat. I could not see any sign of them. I was the only man who had made it to shore.

I was wet and hungry and alone. All I had was a knife and a pipe and a little tobacco in a box. I walked away from the shore and found

a spring of fresh water. I had some to drink. Night was coming. Were there any men or animals on the island? I could not tell. A large tree grew near the spring. I climbed up into its branches. I was so tired that I fell fast asleep.

When I woke up the next day, the storm was over. The sea was quiet. To my surprise, the ship had been washed close to the island. It was resting on sand. We should have stayed on the ship, I thought. Then they would all still be alive.

Then I saw the boat we had used to get away from the ship. It had been washed on shore. But it was too big for me to row by myself.

The ship was full of things I could use. I wanted to get them. I swam out to the ship. Then I pulled myself on deck with a rope that was over the side. On the ship I found bread, cheese, and corn. I also found guns, shot, two old swords, and some gunpowder. Best of all, I found a box of tools.

But how would I get these things back to the island? I made a raft by roping together pieces of wood. I put some things on it. Then I rowed to shore. I took the things off and went back to get more.

This time I took two bags of nails and some axes. I also took seven more guns, and all the clothes I could find.

Near the shore I made a little tent from one of the sails. Inside I put all the things that needed to be kept covered.

In the next two weeks, I went back to the ship 11 times. I put everything on my raft that I could carry. I was happy to see the ship's dog and two cats. I took them, too. I also found some money. I smiled to myself when I saw the money. What good would it do me on this island? One knife, I thought, was better than all the money on the ship. But I took it and put it in a piece of sail.

As I rowed back to the island, a storm came up. I went into my tent and went to sleep. In the morning, the ship was not there. It had gone down in the storm.

2 On the Island

Now I had to build a better place to live. I needed four things. I needed fresh water. I needed to be out of the sun. I needed to be safe from men or animals. And I needed a place where I could see if a ship came by.

I found a good spot on the side of a hill. Here I put up a big tent. I put two rows of heavy posts into the ground around the tent. They were made from trees and were almost six feet high. I made points on the tops. It was very hard work to cut these posts. It was also hard to get them into the ground. But I did it.

The posts ran all around the tent. I did not leave room to get in and out. That would not be safe. I did something better. I made a short ladder to go over the top of the posts. When I was inside, I took the ladder in after me. This way I was all fenced in. I took all of my things inside the fence. I took my food, my guns, and all the other things from the boat.

Every day I went out with my gun. I wanted to see if there was anything I could hunt for food. I found that there were goats on my island. But they ran so fast that they were hard to shoot. One day I killed a mother goat. She had a little kid next to her. It made me very sad to kill her. When the mother fell, the kid stayed by her side. I carried the mother goat home, and the kid followed me. I wanted to tame the kid, but it would not eat anything. I had to kill it, too. These two goats gave me enough meat for a long time.

I felt sad all alone. I wondered if any ships would go by. Would I always have to live on this island? One day I was walking along the shore thinking such thoughts. Yes, you are sad, I thought. But what about the others? There were 14 men in the boat. Where are the 13 others? Why were they not saved? Is it better to be here or there?

Then I felt lucky. I was alive. I had a place to live. I had guns and gunpowder. I had tools to work with.

I had been on the island 12 days. "How will I know the day and the year?" I asked myself. So, I put a large post into the ground. Every day I cut a new line on it. After every six lines, I made one long line. This way I could count the days and weeks.

I did not have all the tools I needed. The posts for my fort were very heavy. Sometimes it took me two days to cut down a tree. It took another day to drive the post into the ground. But I did not care how long anything took. I had nothing but time. The one thing I did every day was to look for food.

One day I sat down with a pen and paper. I had taken them from the boat. I began to write the bad and good things about being on the island.

BAD	GOOD
I am on an island. No one will ever find me.	But I am alive. The other men were all killed.
I am alone. I have no one to talk to, or be with.	But I am not hungry. I can find food here.
I could not hold out long if savage men or animals come after me.	But I am on an island where I can see nothing to hurt me.

After writing this down, I felt better. And I began to see how I could live better, too.

First I would make a table and a chair. I did not know anything about tools or building things. But soon I found that I could make anything I needed. It took time. If I wanted a board, I had to cut down a tree. Then I made it straight on both sides with my axe. I could make only one board from a whole tree. But, as I said, I had lots of time. I liked making things.

My things were all over the fort. I needed a place to put them. I dug a cave in the rocks behind my tent. Then I put boards up along one side of the cave. I kept all my tools and nails on them. I banged sticks into the other sides of the cave. These were to hold my guns and other things.

After some time, I had everything in its right place. Then I began to write in a book about

each of my days. I give some of it here to show what my days were like.

November 5, 1659. I went hunting with my dog and shot a wild cat. I could not eat it, but the skin was soft. I save the skins of all animals I shoot. They can be used for making clothes.

November 13. It rained today and I was glad to see it. It was not so hot on the island after the rain. But I was afraid that the rain might wet my gunpowder. When the rain stopped, I put the gunpowder into little boxes. It would be safe there.

November 18. Today I found a tree in the woods. It had very hard wood. I cut off a piece and took it home. With my axe I made it into a shovel. Every morning I go out hunting. Almost every day I can bring home something to eat.

December 27. Killed a small goat and hurt another in the leg. I caught the one that was hurt. I took care of her until she was better. Soon she became very tame. After a while, she would not go away. So I thought about trying to keep

11

my own goats. This way I will have food even after my gunpowder is all gone.

January 1, 1660. These last few days have been very hot. I have found many goats on the island. But it is hard to get close enough to them to shoot. Tomorrow I will bring my dog to hunt them down.

January 2. I took the dog and set him on the goats. They all turned to face the dog. He ran away from them.

I went hunting every day I could. I found a kind of wild bird like our chicken at home. I took some home to tame. When they grew bigger, they got away. But I found their nests and caught the young birds. They were very good meat.

I needed lights at night. So, when I killed a goat, I saved the fat. I put the fat in a little dish. Then I put a piece of string in the dish. Now I had a light. I could see at night.

One morning in June as I walked along the shore, I found a large turtle. It was the first one I had seen on the island. I took it home and cooked it. Inside I found 60 eggs. The meat was very good to eat. I had eaten nothing but goats and birds since I came to the island.

In late June I became sick. At first I just felt cold. Then I felt very warm. For many nights I could not sleep. This lasted about a week. Then I felt a little better. I had nothing to eat, so I went out hunting. I shot a goat. But I was so weak it was hard to carry it home. I stayed sick for another two weeks. I could walk, but I was still weak.

By the end of June I felt better again. From the 4th of July to the 14th, I walked around. I always carried my gun. At first I stayed near the fort. As I felt better, I took longer walks. I planned to stay inside when the rains came again.

3 King of the Island

I had now been on my island for ten months. As far as I could tell, no other men had ever been there before. I wanted to know more about this place. I went for a long walk. I had never gone so far before. I found open fields of grass. I found tobacco growing. And there were many other plants that I had never seen before. Walking along, I found some grapes. I was happy to see them. I could make raisins from the grapes by drying them in the sun.

I did not go back to the fort that night. I got up into a tree and fell asleep there. The next morning I went about four more miles. At the end of this march, I came to a valley. A little spring of fresh water ran down a hill into the valley. The country looked fresh and green. It was very beautiful. I looked at it and thought, I am king of this island. Then I saw orange and lemon trees. They were all wild. They did not have much fruit on them. But I picked a few lemons. They were very good. I made a fine drink with lemons and water.

I wanted to take home a store of grapes and lemons. I knew that the rains were coming. I wanted to be ready for them. I picked the fruit and carried as much as I could. The next time I came, I would bring bags to carry more.

It took me two days to get home. By that time, the grapes were not good to eat. But the lemons were still good.

The next day I went back with two bags. When I came to the grapes, I saw that many of them were gone. Some wild animals ate them, I think. But what they were I could not tell.

I knew that I could not carry the grapes home. They would not be good to eat when I got there. So I took some grapes and tied them on high branches of trees. There they would dry in the sun and I would have raisins. I carried some lemons back with me.

In about three weeks, the grapes were dry. I now had a lot of raisins. I took them down from the trees. It was a good thing I did. The rains began in a few days. And wet raisins would not be good to eat. I would have lost the best part of my winter food.

It began to rain on August 14. It rained every day until about October 15. Sometimes it came down so hard that I could not leave my fort for days. I did not want to get sick again.

But I went out to hunt two or three times. One day I killed a goat. Another day I found a large turtle. My breakfast was a large dish of raisins. For lunch I had some goat or turtle meat. Dinner was a few turtle's eggs.

At this time, my little family got bigger. One of my cats had run away. She was gone for a long time. I thought something had happened to her. But one day she came home with three kittens. The kittens looked just like their mother. Soon there were too many cats around. I had to kill some of them.

One full year had gone by since I had come to my island. I thanked God for keeping me alive and for giving me food. I was eating well, but I missed having bread. I had found some wheat and rice on the boat. Now I wanted to plant them.

I dug up a piece of ground with my shovel and planted my seeds. But I did not plant them all. I saved some of each kind of seed. This way, if nothing grew, I could try again.

It was lucky that I did. Not one seed grew. The ground was too dry and there was little rain. So, I waited until February and planted the rest of them. This time I found a better spot. It rained in March and April. I had a very good garden.

I had to make my grain into flour. At first I tried to find a rock that I could cut into a bowl. But I had no tools that could cut stone. Then I got a piece of hard wood. With my axe and with fire, I made a round hole in the piece of wood. Then I found a heavy stick. I put my grain in the bowl. Then I pushed the end of the stick on it. In this way, I made flour.

There were many parrots on my island. I wanted to catch one for a pet and teach it to talk, but they were hard to catch. One day I knocked a parrot down with a stick. I took it home, but it was years before I could make him talk. He learned to say my name and a few other words.

I made a canoe by cutting down a large tree and digging it out. It took many months of hard work. I was very pleased with it. It was big enough to carry many men. But it was so heavy that I could not get it into the water. I tried all kinds of things, but nothing worked. It was just too big.

Four years went by. I thought about what I would do if I did not have tools. Thank God I had guns to hunt with and a knife to cut things

with! So, even though I was all alone, I felt lucky.

My clothes were wearing out. So, I made new ones from goatskins. At the same time I made an umbrella to keep off the sun and rain.

Five years went by. Every year I planted my wheat. I made raisins from wild grapes. Every day I hunted goats or turtles.

But now I wanted to sail around my island. I began to make another boat. It was hard work. And it took me almost two years. I made a sail from pieces of the ship's old sail.

On November 6, I set out. As I would be gone for a few days, I took some food. The island was longer than I thought. At the end of the first day I went on shore. A big wind came up. It blew for two days. I was very tired and went to sleep under a tree. But a voice woke me—a voice calling my name. "Robin, Robin, Robin Crusoe, poor Robin Crusoe!" it called. "Where are you, Robin Crusoe? Where are you? Where have you been?"

At first I was very scared. But when I opened my eyes, I saw my parrot sitting on a branch. Then I knew who was calling my name. I wondered how he flew so far from home. But I was very happy to see him. I carried him home with me.

Another year went by. I could now make all kinds of things. I even made a new pipe so that I could smoke. I made baskets. When I killed a goat or turtle, I could carry it back in a basket. I also made big baskets to hold my corn. I could make almost everything I needed— but not shot for my guns. After I had been on my island 11 years, I was running out of shot. When it was gone, I could no longer shoot goats. I tried to catch some live goats, but I could not. I dug some deep holes in the ground and covered them with leaves. At first I could catch nothing. But one morning, I found a large goat in one hole. In another were three kids.

The big goat was very wild and I let him go. But I kept the kids. I built a large pen to keep them in. I gave them some rice to eat. They became tame.

In about a year and six months, I had 12 goats. In two years, I had 43. I found I could also milk the goats. From the milk I made butter and cheese. As I ate I thought about my first day on the island. At that time I was afraid I would go hungry. Now I ate like a king. I was king of the island.

Every day I walked up the hill to look at the sea. I put on a big cap made of a goatskin. The rest of my clothes were goatskin, too. Even my shoes were made of big pieces of goatskin. At one time I let my beard grow a foot long. Now I kept it short.

I now had two homes on the island. One was the fort where I lived. All my things were there. The posts had taken root and were

growing into trees. The fort could not be seen.
My other place was near my field of corn and
the goat pen. Here I kept my tent. This was
near the place where I kept my boat. I never
went very far in the boat because the winds
and tides scared me.

4 Cannibals on the Island

One day something happened that surprised me. I was walking to my boat. In the sand I saw a man's footprint. I stopped. I listened. I looked around. I walked up a hill to look more. But I could hear or see nothing. I went back to look at the footprint. I wanted to make sure I had really seen it. It was still there, a man's footprint in the sand. I tried to find other footprints, but there was only one. As I walked home I looked behind me every two or three steps. It seemed as though every tree was a man.

I ran into my fort like a scared rabbit. That night I could not sleep. How could anyone have come on my island? What brought him here? Why was there only one footprint? Had some people come over from the mainland? Did they find my boat?

If this were so, they could kill me. Even if they could not find me, they could take my corn. They could carry off my goats. Then I would not have any food. I could not live without my corn and goats.

But in a few days I was not afraid any more. I left my fort and began to look around again. My goats were hungry. I had to feed and milk them. I told myself that I was scared because I had lived alone for 15 years. In all that time I had never seen another man.

Another two years went by. Once, as I was out walking, I thought I saw a boat very far away. But I could not be sure. As I came down a hill I saw something on the shore. The sand was covered with the bones of men. A fire had been made and a 'round hole dug in the sand. This was a sign of cannibals—men who ate other men. They had come on my island. Here they

killed and ate men they had caught. I became sick and turned away. I was glad that I lived on the other side of the island. The cannibals would never see me or my fort.

I had been on my island for 18 years. For the next two years I stayed close to my fort and tent. I did not even go to look after my boat in all this time. I was afraid that I might meet the cannibals.

I did very little shooting. I was afraid they might hear the noise if they were on the island. But I always carried my gun and a sword with me. Once I thought I would dig a hole where the cannibals made their fire. Then I would put gunpowder under the sand. When they built their fire, the gunpowder would blow up and kill them. I liked this plan. But I didn't want to use up my gunpowder this way.

My next thought was to find a good place to hide. With my three guns, I could kill two or three with every shot. Then with my sword and pistols I could kill even 20 cannibals. I liked this plan so much that I even dreamed of it.

I found a place on the side of a hill where I could hide. I kept three guns there as well as my pistols. Every morning I went to the top of the hill. It was about three miles from my fort. There I would watch for any boats coming near my island. But after three months, I never saw one boat, even with spyglasses.

As more time went by, I had other thoughts about the cannibals. I asked myself: why should I kill them if they do not hurt me? They think it is all right to kill a man they catch in a fight. But that does not make them bad men. This is what they believe. And I told myself I would not hurt them if they let me alone.

For a year I did not even watch for their boats. But I moved my boat to the east side of the island. No one could find it there.

Most of the time I stayed in my fort. I looked after my goats and gave them food. I still did not want to make smoke around my fort. But I could not live there without baking bread or cooking meat.

One day when I was cutting down some trees I found a big cave. Inside it was very dark. I walked in. There I saw two bright eyes looking at me. I ran out as fast as I could.

Then I told myself, you have lived alone on an island for 20 years. Don't be afraid.

I set a stick on fire and ran into the cave. I heard a noise and stepped back. My hair stood on end, but I kept going. By the light of the

fire I saw an old goat on the ground. Now I looked around inside the cave. It was about 12 feet high. The next day I came back with lights made from goat fat. Part of the cave was so small that I could not stand straight. I had to walk on my hands and knees. But the cave was good and dry. So, I hid my shot and some of my guns in the cave.

The old goat died the next day. I dug a hole in the cave and covered him up. He didn't smell very good.

I had now been 23 years on the island. Sometimes it seemed to me that I would die there. But I was quite happy. I had my parrot to talk to. My dog lived with me for 16 years and he had been a good friend. My old cats had died a long time ago. They were the great-grandmother and great-grandfather of the cats I now had. I also kept two or three kids in my "family." There were also some tame birds that I kept.

It was December. But it was summer on my island. I was busy in my fields. One morning I went to work before the sun came up. I was surprised to see the light of some fire on the shore. It was about two miles away, but on my side of the island.

I ran back to my fort, pulling the ladder after me. I put shot in all the guns and waited inside my fort. But after sitting for a time, I had to see what was happening. I climbed up a hill with my spyglass and lay down on the ground. Soon I saw them—the first men I had seen for 23 years. There were 10 cannibals dancing around a small fire. Their two boats were on

the sand. After a while, they got into their
boats and rowed away. I put down my guns
and sword and ran toward the shore. It was
covered with bones that the cannibals had left.
I was so angry that I thought about killing
them when they came again. I didn't care how
many there would be.

A year and three months went by before I saw more cannibals. But in that time I did not sleep well. I had bad dreams. One stormy night I was reading my Bible when I heard a gun fired. The sound seemed to come from the sea. I jumped over my ladder and went to the top of the hill. Then I heard another shot. That must be a ship, I thought. There is something the matter. The men are firing their guns as a signal.

I brought together all the dry wood I could find and made a big fire. The wind blew hard, but the fire was bright. Then I heard the sound of another gun, followed by others. I put wood on the fire all night long until the day came. I saw something at sea, very far off. I watched it all day long, but it did not move. I ran toward the far end of the island. Then I saw a ship. It had not seen the rocks in the water and had run into them.

I waited to see if anyone was saved. But there was no one. Oh! I thought. If only one had been saved! Just one man that I could have talked with. But it was not to be. I could see no sign of anyone in the water or on the ship.

I wanted to take my boat out to the ship to see what I might find. From my fort I took some bread, a pot of water, and some raisins.

I sailed into the sea in the big waves. It took me a long time to get to the wreck. It was sad to see. When a dog on the ship saw me, he started to bark. I called him and he jumped into the water to come to me. I took him into my boat and gave him some bread and water. He was very hungry.

The first thing I saw on board was two men in one of the rooms. They were dead. Then I found two big trunks, a shovel, and a pot. I put them in my boat.

The next morning I opened the trunks. Inside was a lot of money. I could not use the money. But I carried it to my cave and hid it there. I put my boat away where it belonged and went back to my fort.

One night in March it was raining outside. I was trying to sleep. I did not feel sick. But I could not go to sleep. I thought about England. I thought about the island—I had been here 24 years. I wondered what would happen to me if the savages caught me. Then I wondered if I could sail to the mainland in my boat. Maybe I would meet a ship and they would save me.

After thinking like this for a while, I fell asleep. I dreamed that I was going out one morning as I always did. I saw two boats and 11 cannibals landing on the shore. They had another man with them. They were going to kill and eat him. All at once, the man jumped and ran away. In my dream he ran into the trees to hide. I was there watching. When he came close, I got up and smiled at him. He made signs that I should help him. I took him to my cave. He would work for me.

This man, I dreamed, could show me the way to the mainland. He will tell me where to sail my boat. He will know which places are all right and which are not.

And then I woke up. I felt very happy. I thought that this was the only way I could ever get off my island. If I could catch one of the savages, he might help me.

5 Friday

Almost two years went by before the savages came back. One morning I saw seven canoes on shore. I could not see the people. But I thought there would be 20 or 30 of them. This time they were very close. How could I fight so many? I went back to my fort and got my guns ready. Then I went up the hill where I had built a fence; I had more guns there. I saw with my spyglass that there were about 30 cannibals. They were dancing around their fire.

The cannibals took two men to the fire. They hit one of them on the head with a piece of wood. He fell down. The other man started running very fast. He was running right at me. It was just like my dream. I was afraid that all the savages would run after him. Then they would find me. But only three of them came after him. I could take care of three, I thought. I can save that poor man.

I ran down the hill and saw the first cannibal. I did not want to shoot my gun. So I hit him on the head and knocked him out. As I turned, I saw another cannibal. He was going to shoot an arrow at me. I had to shoot my gun. He fell dead. When the last one heard the shot, he turned and ran away.

I saw the man who had run away from the cannibals. I made signs for him to come to me. He came a little way, then stopped. I called to him and made more signs to show him I was his friend. I smiled at him and soon he was close to me. He laid his head on the ground and put my foot on his head. This was his sign that he was my prisoner.

I helped him up and smiled again. I wanted him to know I was his friend. But there was work to do. The cannibal I had hit with my gun was waking up. I pointed to him, and my new friend said some words to me. Though I did not understand them, they were good to hear. This was the first time I had heard a man's voice in 25 years!

The cannibal was now sitting up in the grass. My friend pointed to my sword and I gave it to him. He ran over to the cannibal and cut off his head in one blow.

But he could not see how I killed the other cannibal. He made signs to me to let him go look at him. I did. When he came close, he turned him to one side and then the other. But he did

not understand guns. He was surprised that the man was dead. Then he picked up the man's bow and arrows and came back.

I made a sign for him to follow me. I was afraid more cannibals would come. He made a sign that he would cover the two dead men with sand. This way they would not be seen by the rest. He dug two holes in the sand with his hands. He put the two cannibals in the holes. Then he covered them up.

I took him to my cave on the far side of the island. There I gave him bread and raisins. I also gave him a lot of water to drink. He was tired. I made a sign for him to lie down and sleep. I showed him where I sometimes used to sleep. He lay down and was soon asleep.

I watched him while he was asleep. He was an Indian from the mainland. He was tall and was light brown in color. He had fine teeth. He woke up in about 30 minutes and came out of the cave. I was milking the goats outside. When he saw me, he ran up to me. He put his head on the ground near my feet. He put my right foot on his head. I knew what he was doing. He was telling me that he would work for me as long as he lived.

35

I began to teach him how to talk with me. I let him know his name would be Friday. That was the day I saved him from the cannibals. I told him how to say "yes" and "no."

I put some milk in a jar and had some to drink. Then I gave the jar to him to drink. I also gave him bread to put into the milk. He made signs that it was very good.

We stayed in the cave all night. Early the next morning, I told him to come with me. We went by the place where he had covered the two men with sand. He made signs that we should dig them up and eat them. I was very angry. I made him see that this would make me sick. We went to the top of the hill to see if the cannibals were still around. But they had all gone. I wanted to make sure this was not a trick. We took guns and a sword and went to the shore. The place was covered with bones. Friday told me they had brought four men to eat. We made a fire. Then we put all the bones into the fire.

After this I took him to my fort. I gave him some clothes, for he did not wear any. First he put on some shorts that I got from the ship. I made him a short coat of goatskin and gave him a cap of rabbit skin. At first he did not like to wear clothes. He said everything was too small and hurt his arms. But after a while he took to them very well.

I thought about where Friday should live. I didn't want him to stay in the fort, so I made him a tent. This was between my fort and the cave. I fitted a wood door for the mouth of the cave. Every night I put a piece of wood across it. This way, he could not come at me without making a lot of noise.

But I soon learned that I did not need to do all these things. Friday was a good and kind man. He did not want to hurt me at all. He would have died for me.

I was very happy to have him on the island. I would teach him many things. First, I would teach him English. Then he could understand me. He wanted to learn. He was pleased when he could understand what I said. Now my days began to be happy. It is good to have a friend, I said to myself. Now I do not care if I always have to live on the island.

Friday was not used to eating the meat of animals. He was used to eating men. I should show him how to eat other meat, I thought. I took him out to the woods one morning. I went with the plan of finding a kid and killing it.

On the way, we saw one. I held Friday by the arm. "Stand still," I said. I put up my gun, shot and killed one of the kids.

Friday, who had seen me kill the cannibal with a gun, was surprised. He started to shake so much that I thought he would fall. He had not seen the kid I had shot at. He thought I was trying to kill him. He got on his knees and said things I did not understand. But I saw that he was asking me not to hurt him.

I took him by the hand and laughed. Then I pointed to the kid I had shot. I asked him to get it. As he was looking at it, I saw a parrot up in a tree. I called Friday. He looked up. I pointed at the bird and then to my gun. I made him understand that I would shoot and kill that bird. I fired. He saw the parrot fall to the ground. But again he was scared. He was surprised because he did not see me put anything into the gun. I could tell what he was thinking. What was this thing? It can kill a man. It can kill a bird. It can kill anything near or far.

After that, he would not come near the gun for many days. But he would talk to it. He would answer it as though it had talked to him. Then he told me he was asking the gun not to kill him.

We took the kid home. That evening I skinned it and cut it up into pieces. I cooked it in a pot and began to eat some. Then I gave a piece to Friday, who liked it quite well. He was surprised to see me put salt on it. He made a sign that salt was not good to eat. He put a little into his own mouth. Then he made a face. He took a long drink of water.

Now it was my turn. I took some meat in my mouth *without* salt. I made believe I didn't like it. But that did not help. Friday never cared for salt on his food.

I had cooked that meat in a pot with water. I tried something new the next day. This time I cooked a piece of kid over a fire. I put two sticks up, one on each side of the fire. Across the two sticks I set a third stick. I tied the

39

meat to this with string. Then I let the meat turn over the fire. Friday liked this way of cooking very much. He ate the meat and said it was the best food he ever had. He told me he would never eat a man again. I was glad to hear this.

After we ate, I showed him how to bake bread. In a little while, Friday could do everything as well as I.

Now that I had two mouths to feed, I needed more food. I had to plant more corn than I used to. I found a bigger piece of land. Friday and I built a fence around it. He worked hard and he was happy. I told him what the new land was for. We would need more corn for bread because he was with me now. We needed enough for two men, not one. He could understand what I said. He told me that I was working too hard for him. I was doing more for him than for myself. To pay me back, he said, he would work hard for me.

This was the best year on the island. I was very happy. Friday began to talk pretty well. He could understand the names of things. He could understand the places I had to send him. We would talk together all the time. That was good. He was such a kind and good man that I liked him very much.

6 We Plan To Leave the Island

Once I asked Friday if his people were good at war. "Yes, yes," he answered. "We always fight the better."

"How did you get caught then?" I asked him.

He said, "They more many than my people in the place where me was. They take one, two, three, and me. My people fight them in far place where me no was. My people win. There my people take one, two, great many."

"But why didn't your people save you and the others?" I asked.

"They run one, two, three, and me into canoe. My people have no canoe that time."

"Well, Friday," I asked, "what do your people do with the men they take? Do they carry them away and eat them?"

"Yes, my people eats man too, eat all up."

"Where do they carry them?" I asked. "Do they come here?"

"Yes, yes, they come here."

"Have you been here with them?" I asked.

"Yes, I been here," said Friday.

Friday had been with the savages who used to come on shore. We walked over to that part of the island. He knew the place and told me this was where they ate 22 people. He could not count this high, so he laid 22 stones in a row.

I asked him how far it was from our island to the mainland. Were canoes often lost at sea? He told me there was nothing to be afraid of. No canoes were ever lost. But there were strong winds. They blew one way in the morning. Then, in the afternoon, they blew the other way.

I asked Friday many things. I asked about the land, the people, the sea, and the shore. I asked him the name of his people. He told me they were called Caribbees.

As we became better friends, I told Friday my own story. I told him how and when I came to the island. I gave him a gun and showed him how to use it. I also gave him a knife. He was very happy.

I told him about England and how people lived there. I told him about the wreck of my ship and showed him where it happened. Then I showed him the wreck of the small boat that had washed on shore. It was so heavy I could not move it. When he saw the boat, Friday thought for a while. At last he said, "Me see such boat come to place near my people."

At first I did not understand. Then he told me that such a boat had come on shore where he lived. A storm blew it there. Then Friday said, "We save the white mans from die."

"How many?" I asked.

He counted 17. I asked him what became of them. "They live with my people," he answered.

This put new thoughts into my head. I believed that these were the men from the wrecked ship I had seen. They must have landed on that wild shore.

I asked Friday what had happened to them. He said they still lived there. They had been there about four years. The Indians let them alone and gave them food. I asked why they did not kill and eat them. He said, "No, make brother with them. They no eat mans but when make war." Friday's people only ate men who came to fight with them.

I asked Friday, "Would you like to be with your people again?"

"Yes," he said. "I be much glad to be at my people."

"What would you do there?" I asked. "Would you turn cannibal again?"

He moved his head from side to side and said, "No, no. Friday tell them to live good. Tell them to eat corn bread, goat, milk. No eat man again."

Friday said his people had learned much from the men who came in the boat. I asked him if he would go back to his people. Friday smiled and said he could not swim so far. I told him I would make a canoe for him. He told me he would go if I went with him.

I said, "They will eat me if I come there."

"No, no," said Friday. "Me make they no eat you. Me make they much love you." He would tell his people how I had saved him. He told me again how kind they were to the 17 white men.

Now I thought about going across the water. Maybe I could be with those men, who were Spaniards or Portuguese. Together we might find a way to get home. Here I was 40 miles from the shore. I could do nothing myself, or even with Friday, to get back to England.

I thought about this for a few days. I told Friday that I would give him a boat that he could sail home. I showed him the small boat I had made. We both got into it.

I found he was a very good sailor. We went very fast. He could sail the boat better than I ever could. I said, "Well, Friday, shall we go to your people?" He thought the boat was too small to go that far. I told him I had a bigger boat. The next day we went to look at the first boat I had made. It was the one I could not get into the water.

Friday said it was big enough. But the boat could not be used. It had been in one place for 23 years. There were too many holes in it. We thought about building another just like it.

We looked for a big tree to cut down. There were many trees on the island. But we wanted one that grew near the water. This way, we could push it right into the sea when we were finished.

Friday knew what kind of tree we needed. We cut one down. He wanted to use fire to dig out the tree. But I showed him how to dig it out with tools. In about four weeks we had a very fine boat. It took us another two weeks to roll her into the water. When she was in, she could have carried 20 men.

Even though it was a big boat, Friday sailed her very well. He could row and turn the boat as he wished. But I had a plan I did not tell Friday. I was going to give the boat a mast and a sail.

For the mast we cut down a straight tree. I took out some pieces of the old sail that I had saved. From this I made a small sail for our boat. It took another seven weeks to finish my mast and sail.

Friday was surprised to see how well the sail worked. We went so fast. Soon he could sail the boat very well. We hid the boat away in a safe place. In November or December we would think about getting to the mainland.

I had been on the island 27 years. But for the last three of these years I had Friday with me. I thanked God for keeping me alive and for sending me my friend Friday.

7 A Fight with the Cannibals

Friday and I began to store food. We would need it when we sailed to the mainland. I asked Friday to go to the shore to find a turtle. Soon he came running back.

"Over there!" he said. "One, two, three canoe!"

Friday was scared. He thought the cannibals had come to look for him.

"Do not be afraid," I said. "We will fight them. Can you fight, Friday?"

"Me shoot," he said. "But there come many men."

"Our guns will scare them away," I said.

I gave Friday two guns. I took four for myself and two pistols. I also gave Friday a sword.

We went up to the top of the hill. Through my spyglass I saw 21 savages. They had brought three prisoners to eat. I was so angry that I wanted to kill all the cannibals. We went down to the shore. We were very quiet. I told Friday to keep close behind and not to shoot until I said so. Soon we were near the cannibals. I sent Friday up to hide behind a big tree and watch them.

He came back after a minute and said that a fire had been started. The cannibals had already killed one man. Another man was tied up near the fire. It was a man with a beard. In other words, it was a white man. Indians do not grow beards.

"Friday," I said, "you watch me and do just as I do."

We picked up our guns. "Are you ready?" I asked. Friday said he was. We hurried out to the shore. I fired. Friday fired, too. He killed two cannibals and hit three more. I killed one and hit two others. All of the rest of the cannibals jumped up. They did not know which way to turn.

We ran toward the prisoner. We called out and fired our guns as we ran. Some of the cannibals got into their canoes and rowed away. But Friday shot more of them on the shore. I ran to the man who was tied and cut his ropes. He said something to me in Spanish.

I said, "We will talk in a while. But we must fight now. Are you strong enough to fight?" He said he was and I gave him a gun.

In a short while we had killed 17 Indians. The other four got away in a canoe. I jumped into one of the canoes they left. I was going to go after them. But in the canoe I found another Indian. I cut the ropes that tied his hands and feet. He was very weak. He could not stand or even talk.

I called Friday. As soon as he saw the man, he jumped up and down. Friday was so happy that he could not talk for a long time. Then he told me why. This man was his father!

I gave Friday's father some bread and water. I also gave some to the Spaniard. Both men were too weak to walk. Friday and I carried them on our backs to the fort. But we could not get them over the fence. So we made two beds for them outside the fence. They would sleep there until they were strong again.

I was afraid that the four cannibals who got away might come back. They might bring more savages. But Friday's father did not think so. He said that the guns had scared them too much. They did not know how a man could be killed from so far away. The noise of the guns scared them, too. They now believed that anyone who came to the island would be killed.

I was not so sure. I watched for canoes all the time. But they never came. I began to think about going to the mainland again. Friday's father told me his people would be good to me.

I talked to the Spaniard. He told me that his ship had been wrecked in a storm. He and 16 others had gotten to the mainland. There they had lived with Friday's people. But they did not have guns or food. They had no boat and no tools to build one. So, they had no way to get home. They thought they would always have to live with the Indians.

"I could help get us all back home," I said. "You and the 16 others could come here. I have tools and together we could build a big boat. Then we could all sail home on it."

The Spaniard said that he and Friday's father would go back to the mainland. They would ask the men if they wanted to go home.

I told the Spaniard that I would be the leader. The men would have to listen to me. He said that they would. But he asked if I had enough food to feed all these men. We would need even more to put on the boat for our trip home.

This seemed like a good thought. So all four of us started digging and planting. We planted corn and rice. We tamed 20 more goats. The grapes were ready to be picked. We picked them and put them in the sun to make raisins. The raisins could have filled 60 big baskets.

Now we had lots of food. I told the Spaniard that he could go to the mainland. He and Friday's father left in one of the canoes the cannibals had brought. I gave each man a gun and shot. I gave them bread and raisins — enough for them and for the 16 others. And so they left. After 27 years on the island, I might at last go home.

8 The English Ship

Eight days after the Spaniard and Friday's father left, something very surprising happened. I was asleep one morning. Friday ran in and called, "They are come! They are come!"

I jumped up and got dressed. I ran to the shore and looked out over the water. I saw a large ship with a sail coming toward us. It was about seven miles away. These were not the people we were looking for. I did not know who they were.

I sent Friday to get my spyglass. Then I climbed to the top of the hill. The ship had stopped about four miles away. It looked like an English ship to me. Then I saw a small boat coming toward the island.

I was very happy to see the ship. But at the same time I felt that something was not right. First of all, English ships did not come to this part of the world. And there had been no heavy winds or storms to drive them here. If she was really English, then she was up to no good.

Soon I saw a small boat draw near the shore. It was not quite a mile away from where I hid.

It carried 11 men. The first four or five men jumped on shore. Then they brought out three men who were tied up. They must be their prisoners. I could not understand what was happening.

Friday said, "You see? English mans eat prisoner as well as savage mans."

I said, "Do you think they are going to eat them?"

"Yes," said Friday. "They will eat them."

"No, Friday," I said. "I am afraid they will kill them. But they will not eat them."

I wished that the Spaniard and Friday's father were still with us. I wanted to save the three men who were tied. Some of the other men began running around. They wanted to see what was on the island. Now I saw that only the men's hands were tied. But they just sat down on the ground and looked very sad.

I thought of the first time I came on shore. I, too, looked around. I did not know how I would live. I did not know if there were wild animals here.

When the men had come on shore, it was high tide. By now, though, the tide had gone out. Their small boat was left high and dry. Two men were still in the boat. They had been asleep— from drinking too much, I guessed. One of the men in the boat woke up. He saw that the boat was out of the water. He called out to the others. They all came to the boat and tried to push it into the water. But it was too heavy to move.

Then I heard one say, "Let her alone, Jack. We will wait for the next tide." On hearing this, I knew for sure that the men were English.

I knew that the tide would not be that high for ten hours. By then it would be dark. I would watch them and hear as much as I could.

I got myself ready to fight. I told Friday to get some guns for himself. He was now a very good shot. I had two pistols and gave Friday three guns. I also carried a sword.

After a while, many of the men fell asleep. But the three prisoners sat under a tree. They were not too far away from me. Friday and I walked over to them. I called to them in Spanish: "Who are you?"

They jumped at the noise. When they saw me they were afraid. It looked as though they would run away. Then I talked to them in English. "Do not be afraid. You may have a friend even though you do not think so."

"Thank you, sir," said one of the men. "But I am afraid that no man can help us now."

"Maybe I can help you," I said.

"Who are you?" he asked.

"I am an Englishman. I want to help you. This is Friday. He works for me. We have guns, gunpowder, and shot. What is going on here?"

"I was captain of that ship," answered the man. "My men had a mutiny. They almost killed me. Then they left me on shore with these two men. One is my mate. The other is a passenger."

"Where are the others?" I asked.

"Sleeping," he answered. And he pointed to some trees. "I don't want them to hear us talk. If they did, they will kill us all."

"Do they have guns?" I asked. He told me they had two guns. They were both in the boats.

"Leave the rest to me," I said. "I see they are all asleep. It will not be hard to kill them. Or should we take them prisoner?"

The captain said not to kill them, if we did not have to.

"Let us walk in the woods," I said. Soon the trees hid us. "I will help you," I said. "But I must ask you to agree to two things. One, that I am the leader on this island. Two, that you will take Friday and me to England."

The captain agreed to both. Then I took the ropes from their hands. "All right," I said. "Here are guns and shot for the three of you."

As we talked, we heard some of the other men wake up. We saw two of them stand. As soon as they saw us, they cried out. The mate and the passenger fired. One sailor was killed. The other was hit but not killed. He called for help. The captain ran over and knocked him down with his gun. Soon the others saw that they could not get away. The

59

captain said he would not kill them. But they had to agree to help him. He needed help to take the ship from the men still on board. Thy agreed to be on his side. I told the captain to tie their hands and feet. Then we put them up in the cave.

9 Taking the Ship

Now I told the captain my story. I showed him my fort. I showed him the things I had made. He was surprised to see how well I lived on my island.

We talked about getting his ship back. He did not know what to do. There were still 26 sailors on board. They had all taken part in the mutiny. If they were ever brought back to England, they would be killed. But we could not fight 26 men very well.

I said that they would soon wonder where their friends were. They would send another boat to see what had happened to them. If they all brought guns, they would be too strong for us.

Then I had a thought. We must wreck the small boat on the shore. We went to it and took off the guns. We also took off some boxes of food. Then we knocked a big hole in the bottom of the boat.

Now the men on the ship could not use the boat. If they sailed away without it, then we could use it. As we were working, we heard the ship fire a gun. This was a signal to the men on the island. They were our prisoners, so they could not answer. The ship fired a few more times.

With my spyglass I saw them put down another boat. The boat started toward the island. As it came close, I saw that there were about ten men in it. They all had guns.

I gave the spyglass to the captain. He could see the men's faces well. Three of them, he said, were good men. The others were not. He was afraid that they would be too strong for us. Besides, there were still more men on the ship.

"There are seven of us here," I said. "There are Friday and I, you, your mate, and the passenger. And there are two men in the cave you say are good men. We seven will be strong enough for those ten men."

We went to the cave and let the two men the captain believed in go. The others we left tied. I told them that we would kill them if they tried to get away.

The boat from the ship was coming toward us. It was very close now. Soon it came to the shore. The men all got out and ran to the other boat. They were surprised when they got to the boat.

No one was in it. There was a big hole in the bottom.

They shouted for their friends. But no one answered. They shot their guns in the air. Again no one answered. For a while, we were afraid they would go back to the ship. If they sailed off, we would never get away. But they left three men to watch the boat. Then the rest of them went to look for their friends. Now *we* did not know what to do. If we caught the seven men, the others might row back to the ship. We could only wait and see what would happen.

The seven men walked around and called out. Every once in a while, they fired their guns. No one answered. Then they sat under a tree to talk.

The captain had a plan. If all seven men fired their guns again, we could run at them. They would have no time to put more shot in their guns. We could catch them without killing them. This sounded like a good plan. We waited for them to shoot. But they did not fire their guns again.

Then I thought of a plan. I told Friday and the mate to go toward the west for about a mile. I told them to shout as loud as they could. The sailors would think it was their friends. If they answered, Friday and the mate would call out again. But they would not let the sailors see them. And they would keep moving toward the woods.

The sailors got up and went down to the shore. They were just about to get into the boat. Then they heard Friday and the mate call out. They ran along the shore toward the voices. But two men still stayed with the boat.

When the others had gone, the captain and I ran to the boat. One sailor was sitting on the shore. The other was in the boat. The one on shore had been asleep. The captain knocked him down right away. He told the one in the boat to give up or be killed.

The other sailors followed Friday and the mate all over the island. They went from one hill and one woods to another. The sailors were getting tired. They did not even know where they were. They did not know if they could get back to the boat before dark.

Friday and the mate now moved back toward the boat. We had nothing to do but wait for the sailors. After a while, we could hear them coming. We heard them saying how tired they were. That was good news to us.

Soon they came near the boat. They saw that the tide had gone out. And they found that the two men left with the boat were gone. Now they were really afraid. They shouted at each other. They didn't know anything about the island, they said. They could all be killed, they said.

They called out for the two sailors who had stayed with the boat. They got no answer. It was getting dark now. We could see them running around. Sometimes they sat on the shore. Sometimes they ran back to the boat on the sand.

My men wanted to fall on them in the dark. But I did not want to kill them all. And I did not want any of our men to get hurt. The sailors had guns, too.

"Let's wait," I said. "Maybe some will go off one way. And maybe the rest will go another way."

I sent Friday and the captain to go up close to them. Soon three of the men came walking toward Friday and the captain. The first man of the three was the leader of the mutiny. When the three men took a few more steps, the captain and Friday fired. They killed the leader on the spot. The next man was shot and fell down. The other ran away.

As soon as I heard the shot, I marched with eight men. We came on them in the dark. They did not know how many men we were. One of the captain's men called out, "Give up, Tom Smith! Throw down your guns or you will all be killed!"

66

"Where are they? Where are they?" shouted Smith.

"It is our captain," called the man. "He has 50 men with him. Will Frye has been shot. Give up or you will all die."

"Will they hurt us if we give up?" asked Smith.

"I will ask the captain," answered the man.

The captain called out. "Smith, you know my voice. If you give up you will save your lives. All but Will Atkins."

Then Will Atkins cried out, "What have I done, Captain? They have all been as bad as I."

But this was not so. Will Atkins had been the first man to lay hands on the captain. He had tied him up. Then he had said bad things to him.

Soon all the sailors put down their guns and asked not to be killed. We tied them up.

Now we made plans for getting the ship. I told the captain to pick five men from our new prisoners. They were afraid for their lives, so they wanted to help us. We had 12 men:

1. The captain, his mate, and the passenger.
2. The two men from the first boat who had helped us.
3. The other two men from the first boat who had been tied up.
4. The last five we let go.

Friday and I would stay and watch the prisoners.

We went to the boat with a hole in it. We put wood over the hole. Now we had two boats.

The captain made the passenger leader of one. He had four men with him. The captain, his mate, and five more men went in the other boat. They rowed off in the dark.

When they got to the ship it was still dark. The captain told a man to call out that they had found the missing men. Then the captain and his mate climbed up on the deck of the ship. They knocked down two men on the deck with their guns. Soon the others from the boats were on the deck. They closed all the doors to the deck so no one could get out. Then they went to the place where another leader of the mutiny was hiding. The mate shot him in the head. The 12 men had taken the ship!

The captain fired seven guns. This was a signal to me that they had taken the ship. You may be sure I was very glad to hear it. I had sat for a long time waiting for those guns.

10 Home!

I felt very tired and went to sleep. When I woke up in the morning, I heard a man calling my name. I knew it was the captain. I climbed to the top of the hill. There he stood, pointing to the ship. "My dear friend," he said. "There is your ship. She is all yours. So are all of us who belong to her."

I looked out to sea. The ship was not very far away. It was near the place where I had first landed my raft. After 28 years, a ship to take me home!

At first I could not believe my eyes. I sat down on the ground in surprise. Then I looked again. Yes, the ship was still there! The ship that would carry me back to England!

I could not say one word. The captain helped me to my feet. He talked to me in a soft voice. He gave me something to drink. The captain tried to bring me to myself. But I was so happy that I could still say nothing. At last I began to cry. In a little while, I could talk again.

The captain said that he had brought me some things from the ship. He called out to the men in the boat. He told them to bring the things on shore. And what things! First they brought something to drink. Then tobacco and 12 pieces of meat.

Then they brought boxes of flour and some lemons. Best of all were the clothes—shoes, a hat, and a suit. The suit was the captain's, but it was almost new. I had new clothes from head to foot.

For so many years I had been used to my clothes of goatskin. My new clothes felt funny at first. Now I knew how Friday felt when I first gave him clothes to wear.

The captain was wondering what to do with our five prisoners. "Two of them are very bad men," he said. "If I take them on the ship, they will be tied up. When they get to England, they will be killed."

I said that maybe I could get them to agree to stay on the island.

"I would be very glad of that," said the captain.

"I will talk to them," I said.

I went to see them, dressed in my new clothes. I told them that I was the leader on the island. I told them that I knew about their mutiny. "Now," I said, "the ship is in the hands of its captain again. All the other leaders of the mutiny have

been killed. If we take you to England, you will be killed. But you can stay on this island if you wish. You will save your lives and live well here."

They seemed very glad. They said they would stay on the island. They did not want to go to England. The captain acted as if he did not want to leave them. Then I made believe I was a little angry with the captain. I told him they were my prisoners, not his. I had told them that they could stay. I would not go back on my word.

Again the prisoners seemed very glad. I took the ropes off their hands and feet. I told them I would leave them guns, shot, and gunpowder. I would also tell them how to stay alive on the island.

I told the captain I would stay one more night on the island. He went back to the ship, saying he would send a boat in the morning. After the captain left, I told the five prisoners about the island. I showed them my fort. I told them how I had planted corn and made bread. I showed them where the grapes grew and how to make raisins. I told them that the 17 Spaniards would be coming. For them I left a letter. I made them say they would be good to the Spaniards. They said they would be friends.

I left them five guns, three pistols, and a sword. I gave them my gunpowder. I told them about my goats. "They must be milked every day," I said. "You can make your own butter and cheese."

I told them every part of my own story. I said I would ask the captain to leave more gunpowder and some seeds.

The next day the boat came for me. I got on board the big ship. I carried on board my goatskin cap, my umbrella, and one of my parrots. I took the money I found on the Spanish wreck.

We did not sail that day. Early the next morning, two of the five prisoners swam to the ship's side. They cried out and said the other three men would kill them. They asked the captain to take them on board. He could even kill them if he wished, they cried.

The captain said he could do nothing, without me. He looked at me. Again, the men asked to be taken on board. They told me that they would be good. At last the captain said they could come on board. They hurried up the ropes and jumped on deck. At first, the other sailors hit them. But they turned out to be good men after all.

The tide was up. The boat was rowed to shore for the last time. It carried the gunpowder and seeds for the three men left on the island. The captain also sent them their clothes and sea trunks.

And so I left my island. It was the 19th of December, 1686. I had been there 28 years, 2 months, and 19 days. In June, 1687, we got to England. I had not been home for 35 years.

I went to York, where I was born. My father and mother were dead. I found two sisters and the children of one brother. But soon I got very good news from Brazil. My farm had done well all these years. A good man ran the farm for me. He had saved up a lot of money for me.

Friday stayed with me in England. We often talked of our days on the island. We wondered about Friday's father and the Spaniards. Did they ever come back to the island? And the three men we had left there—how were they living?

After a while I grew tired of England. I wanted to go to sea again. I thought of going back to my island. I wanted to see what it looked like. I wanted to see what the men had done to it. At last, I could stay in England no longer. I took off on another ship. But that, as they say, is another story.